About

Originally from Litherland in Liverpool, Linda left home for London at 18; embarking on a long career in recruitment, sales, and was a small business owner. She now lives with her husband, son and their two dogs in the beautiful Gloucestershire countryside. This is her first publication of poems that focuses solely on braving the stigma that surrounds our mental health challenges. Her passion for writing is now more than a hobby.

Out of My Mind

Linda Thorne

Out of My Mind

Olympia Publishers
London

www.olympiapublishers.com
OLYMPIA PAPERBACK EDITION

A CIP catalogue record for this title is
available from the British Library.

ISBN: 978-1-78830-473-3

First Published in 2020
Olympia Publishers
Tallis House
2 Tallis Street
London
EC4Y 0AB
Printed in Great Britain

Dedication

For all those who suffer in silence, know you're not alone.

Acknowledgements

Firstly, to my husband, for his belief in me; my son, whose driven and wise soul is so inspiring; my family, especially my two musketeers whose support and encouragement always outshine my doubt; and, not least, the lovely people who have allowed me into their world and are encapsulated within many of these poems. We have shared such truths and flung open our closet doors. Thank you.

FOREWORD

For all those suffering in silence, know you are not alone.

Bipolar 2 and me. Though diagnosed as borderline (a word I clung onto for dear life), I was embarrassed to admit to anyone outside of my inner sanctum of family members that I had this condition at all. For many years undiagnosed, I fought constantly with myself; anxiety attacks, extreme mood swings with high highs and lows, these were aspects of me I just lived with, as did those around me who loved me, unconditionally, but at those low times, I know it hurt.

Eventually, I faced my fear and sought the professional help I needed. Wow! what a relief, I was normal after all, I had a condition and I was fixable. I do still acknowledge elements of my condition; only now, well managed, I understand them and accept they are a part of me, but more importantly I'm no longer defined by them.

But hey, it wasn't all bad news, my condition stretched me, I achieved as much success in my life as I did drama, my condition drove and inspired me to do things I may never have contemplated, at times I was fearless and that was amazing.

Once I was brave enough to talk about my condition I found within my own circle of acquaintances, friends, and even family members that there was a variety of mental health challenges going on all around me, I was unaware that these beautiful people were fighting a silent battle of their own, all different yet like me embarrassed or fearful of rejection or ridicule to speak out or to ask for help. What a privilege to have shared experiences with them and that they have allowed me to encapsulate them here in Out of my Mind, they too wanted to be a part of something that could possibly inspire someone else to reach outside of their silent battle, to feel the freedom and relief that sharing and getting help brings. If this poetry inspires, helps start the conversation or comforts, then it was most certainly worth coming out of the closet.

According to the World Health Organisation, one in four people in the world will be affected by mental or neurological disorders at some point in their lives. Around 450 million people currently suffer from such conditions, placing mental disorders among the leading causes of ill health and disability worldwide.

Around the world people are fighting the stigma that once surrounded challenges in mental health, through education, openness and support.

Our mental health is as important as our physical health.

COLOURS

When you take a look at me,
I wonder what you see
a warm and friendly person,
yes that definitely is me
I hide away my colours,
the ones you wouldn't like
for I'm afraid they'll scare you
and I need you in my life
I will always let you see
the confidence of yellow
and you will think I'm balanced,
cheerful, even mellow
but deep inside the colour black
is waiting, biding time
to fill my head with nonsense
of a very hurtful kind
It takes away my shine within,
it suffocates my nice
it's stronger than my rainbow
and the brightness of my white
I try not to let you see me
when black is taking hold
I hide away unchallenged,
allow this darkness to unfold
I know you cannot help me,
you could never understand
how this warm and friendly person
cannot shine upon demand

I fear you would not love me,
that I could be so sad
you'd scold me and just tell me,
things can never be that bad
To me it's real, unshifting,
I'm scared and I'm alone
if I could just paint over
this hateful colour in my soul
I long to be just like you,
so steady and controlled
I long to have you hug me
when my blackness takes a hold
but I can never tell you
I'm so needy in this way
because I'm really frightened,
you'll just want to walk away
I'll pretend that when my black is gone,
and my rainbow reappears
that all's been well and I can quell
the falling of my tears.

'The sun always follows
the storm to deliver the
rainbow

Have patience in the storm'

YOU'RE BEAUTIFUL

You carry with you every ill
and wear your battle scars
forgetting you're courageous
and just how beautiful you are
Low self-esteem and times of doubt
shadow your resolve
yet I'm full of admiration
for the battles you've resolved
You do not take, you do not judge,
you do not comprehend
the beauty in your nature
and your loyalty as a friend
I love you for your fortitude,
I value time that's ours
but most of all
I wish you knew how beautiful you are.

'Your worth is beyond value
don't sell yourself short'

HIDDEN

Today I'm down, just want to cry,
I'll sob my sadness out
please can someone tell me
what this illness is about
How selfish this condition is,
how random, how unfair
how dare I even ask someone
to comfort me or care
You can't view this thing that brings me down,
it's not obvious to me
how to stop this lifeless form
from taking something you can't see
You can't tend me with a bandage,
you can't offer me a cure
you can't sympathise or recognise
my symptoms that's for sure
The symptom is my sadness,
trapped within my head
it cripples and denies me,
so things are left unsaid
How serious this condition,
how impossible to share
I'm embarrassed to admit
this invisible despair
for it does not grow
and it does not spread
just stays there hidden
deep within my head
I wish it gone or better still
I wish it never was
for it's taken something from me,
a part forever lost
Depression is an illness
and should be treated with respect
hidden makes it harder
to acknowledge or accept.

'Things get much better when we stop hiding from ourselves'

IT'S OK

Let me take the hair from your eyes
my hand caress your lovely face
you're suffering today, it's no surprise
but you're safe here in my embrace
Your strength today has been put aside
take your rest from the human race
you're not alone, I'm by your side
till fears subside and peace in place.

'to embrace and be embraced is healing'

THE MONSTER IN MY HEAD

It's gone, I think I'm free at last, the sun is shining down,
that monster in my head has finally gone to ground
I'm thinking really clearly, there's nothing now to fear,
the monster in my head has gone, It's nowhere near
I'm so lucky, it's amazing, I'm enjoying every day
I'm seeing that there's nothing now standing in my way
Oops, I think I hear it, I think it's getting near
I think it's reinstating my dread and all my fear
I'm silent now, I'm standing with this monster in my head
telling me I'm captured and filling me with dread
I see now I am nothing, I am useless to defend
my mind is taken over by this undeserving friend
Yes, I know it very well, I have known it all along
my past and present meet with it, my future too is gone
I plot to kill this nightmare, this dread within my core
what tools are mine in battle are the words that I implore
I beg myself to push it out, to close this open door
to prevent it penetrating my life, my every thought
It's depleting me of rationale, it's stripping me of pride
it's obsessive and determined, with no place I can hide
It's convinced me I am worthless, less than barely there
convinced me I am nothing, this is more than I can bare
But somewhere in the ether
someone's calling out my name
reminding me I'm human, I'm precious and I'm sane
Now the time is passing, this imposter now retreats
I find myself in balance with the world and too with me
To fight this is to win, if only battles not the war
for each day that I survive it
makes me stronger than before

'It really is OK not to be OK
because it passes'

LOVE YOURSELF

You love everyone, you give so openly and real
but you leave yourself out and ignore how you feel
You give without taking and push for others success
yet ignore all your talents and potential you supress
You would walk up a mountain to save someone else
but you won't take a step to give love to yourself
You hurt when others suffer and carry their pain
and accept that you're forgotten when they're happy again
You give of your time when time is not yours
and will never reveal times, when your need is more
You will always say yes when you should really say no
but your heart is so big it's a word you don't know
You're just far too busy caring for everyone else
I just wish you'd give time to give love to yourself.

'YOU deserve your love too'

DON'T DEFINE ME

Don't define me by my illness, this isn't who I am
just a little understanding to see me if you can
It isn't contagious, you won't pick it up from me
it doesn't stop me loving, or being loved you see
a little chemical imbalance that alternates my mood
but you'd hardly ever notice as I keep it in control
I've lived with this condition for many, many years
undiagnosed I just supposed, yes, that I was weird
I admit that things got tricky, affecting those I love
they didn't understand they couldn't solve it with a hug
or equally control me when I was fuelled with energy
creatively inventing with such intensity
I learned to hate or love myself enough to ask for help
my diagnosis a relief and an investment in my health
I've removed that painful stigma I have chosen to accept
that I have met with challenge won
and gained my self-respect
so don't define me by my illness because it's under mental health,
I'm just dealing with imbalance
in my normal balanced self.

'In a world full of labels
be your own brand'

YOUR WORTH

You see yourself as less than them
if you only knew your worth
your value more fourfold and ten
from the moment of your birth
The breath of life a gift to you
you a gift to life on earth
so never doubt your value here
and never doubt your worth.

'You are your biggest gift,
no one else has a you'

MENTALLY ELITE

What happens that makes you anxious
leaves you feeling weak
If not a something then a someone,
perhaps one of the mentally elite
It seems they are superior;
it seems they are at rest
when they find that you're inferior,
infers that they're the best
You inflate their giant ego
and support their handmade pedestal
You make them very credible;
they win, when sending you hysterical
you believe it's you that's horrible,
you that causes pain
it's not hard for them
to disregard your torment or your shame
Vulnerabilities are ridiculed,
they don't recognise they have any
they can laugh at your expense;
they think they are exemplary
Relax, it's their judgment a toxin undeniable
it's the only thing about them
that's always so reliable
It's not you, it just seems you had to meet
that perfect human being, one of the mentally elite.

'Those who look for faults in others
reveal that major fault in themselves'

UNNOTICED

Amongst the clothes that filled the space
on tables long and short
were toys now old, unwanted
that my attention caught
I found a teddy lying there
with missing eyes and ears
it reminded me of one such toy
I'd lost along the years
I saw in him reflections
of my own life now gone by
old and left unnoticed,
I accept it with a sigh
But I could still be valued,
if someone stopped to see
just a little bit of time well spent,
could be an hour spent with me
I used to have a busy life,
but with old age loneliness arrived
losing friends and family moved,
it seems only I survived
I struggle on to find things
Just to entertain myself
and when the blues attach themselves
I Know it's no good for my health
so, when I'm feeling able,
I dress in my smart familiar way
I go out and chat to strangers,
and it brightens up my day.

'Sometimes the biggest act of kindness
is giving a little of our time'

DEMON DRINK

I think I'm hilarious, you tell me I'm nasty and gruff
I'll tease and I'll test you, till you've had enough
Your patience I'll break, as good as you are
I've potential of killing all that is ours
The love that you give me I toss back at your feet
I hurt and desert all potential in me.
Then suddenly wake you with love undenied
and beg your forgiveness, losing my pride
I give you my word it won't happen again
silently knowing that's hard to attain
It starts with a glass, ending up more than a bottle
I'm deluding myself when I cry and I grovel
The devil I blame is my object of love
The drink I desire now a miserable drug
I'm stuck, I'm silently afraid to admit
I don't have the strength to ultimately quit
I'm scared I'm losing your love and your faith
Don't leave me behind I admit my mistake
Help me, I'm dying, I'll do anything for
Honestly…
A drink in my hand before you walk out the door.

'The worst day of recovery
is better than the best day of
addiction'

I was told so by
someone who knows

REACHING YOU

It's taken time to reach you,
you were unwilling to be helped
but patience, time and loving
led to more than I had hoped
Finally, you let me in,
you trusted me with you
the result was overwhelming,
and you could see it too
Your darkest times behind you,
your confidence is clear
your courage and your strength revealed
and finally lost, your fear
I know that going forward,
this may always be with you
but I am here right by your side,
support in all you do.

'Trust is earned by being true to ourselves
as well as being true to each other
Otherwise it doesn't work'

DESPICABLE DEPRESSION

Is anybody out there, is anybody near
can anybody sense my angst, my nervousness, my fear?
I'm alone with my demented crippled brain
I despise this state of mind I question am I sane
I feel unhinged, out of control, the wires within my head
are sparking off each other and filling me with dread
The bright spark you fell upon has shrivelled and is dying
the nice you liked now been replaced
by patheticness and crying
I have no confidence that's what it is,
no self-preserved respect
for I deem that my condition
leaves me nothing to impress
I never learn my lesson when I sink into depression
I always let it strip me of my dignity and strength
It's hard to see the end of it, I hold it with contempt
but I shall live again, I will be back,
my mind in my possession
but I know it hides inside me, despicable depression.

'It's lonely in the dark
What joy when the light appears'

THANK YOU

Thank you for giving me the best of you,
I didn't always see
that you were there when times were bad,
still supporting me
A constant understanding,
with things often hard to comprehend
your encouragement and praise,
of which I could always depend
Your comfort at those times,
more difficult at night
reminding me when out of sorts
that everything's alright
My love for you is total,
my respect for you immense
you're an angel and a blessing
with all that represents.

'Being thankful, means we appreciate
and that's very important'

FIVE MOODS ONE MORNING

Up with the lark, couldn't sleep,
tossed and turned all night
Unrested but by breakfast
I was buzzing industrious delight
Somewhere around ten I was crying,
I didn't know the cause
and by half past I was fretting,
much more anxious than before
Must have been eleven, I was feeling cheerful
and everything was fine
then come midday, well hey,
I'm creativity defined!
Welcome to my world
of ever-changing moods
a whirlwind of emotions
that reasoning eludes.

'Moods are more complex
than being merely unpredictable'

FOOD FOR THOUGHT

That glorious food all colours and spice
that mixture of dishes that always look nice
The texture and smell the longing to taste
the thought of eating, a conflict to face
My mind tells my eyes this is dangerous stuff
It looks good on the plate, but not good enough
for the fear that this food turns my body to fat
Is the reason, I'm not eating any of that
If it goes down, it will have to come out
Bulimia is what I'm talking about
or just don't have it as simple as that
this neglect of myself is a punishing act
I'm just feeling retched by the thought of that food
making me ugly and changing my mood
Unhealthy in body and mind
crying for help, yet help hiding behind.
But this confession, my courage surprises me now
my longing to heal leaves fear subsiding somehow.
My gift to myself is my effort to change
my unhealthy habit my feeling of shame.

'We work at other relationships, why should food be different.'

'Nourishment, healing, self love'

MY MOTHER'S HAND

Mum, as I look back through time
did I hold your hand or did you hold mine?
You held mine first, I hold yours now,
a warm and loving touch
my heart seeps through my fingers,
I love you very much
I close my eyes and realise
no one's hand feels quite the same
I hope I have another chance
to hold your hand again
I take this time so precious
to kiss this hand of yours
and hope the smile you're wearing
means you're holding mine in yours
The bond we have is precious
and to me will always be
my mother's hand so graceful
showed a loving hand to me
Time has passed so quickly,
now time is at a stand
our travelled road made special
by... the holding of your hand.

'A mother's hand
the one you'll always want to
hold
especially when you can't'

IT'S A SCAM

Because today I feel unworthy, doesn't really mean I am
I've been invaded slyly by this international scam
It's a trojan horse that's programmed
to infiltrate my mind
I know there's many people endure a very similar kind
It's an intelligent programme, designed to test my skill
a breach on my security, a wall to block my will
So, while I feel unable or incapable to perform
the simple daily task of getting up, or to conform
I need to take the challenge, reprogram me again
to stop this sly intruder from running through my brain
This scam can target anyone,
some more susceptible than most
an international problem inevitable host's
This brokenness is fixable, a trojan horse can be deployed
by joining in and sharing, this scam could be destroyed
So, every time your hardware comes under this attack
Remember that it's malware, we can always counteract.

'Knowledge is Power'

PEACE, IF ONLY

Peace is a word that conjures up hope
if man can find peace with himself
and the world in his scope
Practice caring without profit
or personal gain
to accept that we're different,
resist causing pain
Reserve our judgement,
then not being judged
Truly care for another's mind,
without it begrudged
If we could share
and not be led by greed
if we accept and respect a man,
regardless of colour or creed
Forgiving and kindness,
acceptance brings peace of mind
from the mind of one person
to the whole of mankind.

'We are all in this together'

THE OTHER SIDE OF ME

The ones I loved the very most
always got my worst
my dysfunction and my anger
caused their confusion and their hurt
My innocents, my victims,
my captives unreleased
my hostages un-salvaged,
their grief beyond belief
My absence or my silence
was no reflection of my love
but the hiding of my other side
that they misunderstood
I was desperate to explain to them,
I had to make it clear
if they could just be patient,
wait for me to reappear
I couldn't do this thing to them,
or matter of fact to me
I knew I needed help,
someone special I could see
My anger, their confusion
sadly was combined
contained and held until I sort,
the help to heal my mind.

'You need to want change to have change'

WRITTEN WORD

If I share with you a secret
of a very private kind
would you laugh at me behind my back,
my faith be undermined?
I've been writing like a demon,
I'll have to do it while I can
before this energy denies me,
of who I really am
I find freedom in my writing,
I engage my mind in rhyme
I could write like this forever,
fill these pages all the time
The focus of my writing
is the focus of my thought
my secret self-embarrassment,
my inward discord
It helps me to explain myself
in many different ways
my disorder can express itself
in each and every phase
A deliberate confession,
a purging of my soul
an honest deposition,
a way to take control.

'if we don't do say or act for fear of
being laughed at

how will we ever know our potential'

HAPPY PLACE

I have journeyed far;
my shame and conflict fade away
I have faced my fears
and battled them slowly day by day
My disorder now not who I am,
no need now to pretend
I no longer feel exposed to harm,
to myself I made amends
I forgave I had a lack of faith
at a time when help was near
I came to accept and understand
my anxiety and fear
Now I pursue my goals realistically,
and allow for days of doubt
I face life characteristically
as me and what I'm about
Imagine for a minute
the lack of fear of losing face
That journey of discovery,
that real and happy place.

'Delight in your own victories
the rewards are truly yours'

DELUSION or PERCEPTION

You're finding it hard, they enjoy your lack of faith,
you're not devious nor cunning,
so you really don't feel safe
They think you cannot see them
planning your demise
they think they have the power complete
and do, to your surprise
It's not safe for you to be there,
living in this way
with someone who takes pleasure
in what they take away.
Perhaps you'll summon courage,
perhaps you'll climb that inner wall
or is it paranoia
and they're not like that at all.

'We can all get paranoid
it's the degree that needs
examination
for our concerns may be
warranted'

PERMISSION GRANTED

I beat myself up
for having a negative reaction
to something or someone
to their dissatisfaction
I forget it's okay
to be angry in a given position
It's my natural reaction
and not my condition
I don't want to stay quiet
when I've something to say
my right to respond,
what I need to convey
So here,
I give myself granted permission
to have my reaction
without any submission
Reminding myself,
it's okay not to be
the submissive,
peace keeping, agreeable me.

'You don't need the validation of
others
to have your own reaction or
opinion'

WE WILL

We may be down
but we're not out
We may think we've failed,
yet we must hold out
We may feel broken
but heal we must
Rise up
when our spirit's crushed
We may lose
yet not all be lost
Start again,
count not the cost
We may bend
but we will not break
We may feel fear,
yet fearlessness awake
We will not hide,
we will not run
We will stand tall
and we will overcome.

'You breathe, so you're not beat'

IF I COULD BE DIFFERENT

If I could be different who would I be
what would I change in the character that's me
what don't I like, what would I lose
so many facets, which ones would I choose
and what is it making me think that I should
change any of me so what if I could?
If I was any different it wouldn't be me
and the person you're seeing, you'll no longer see
perhaps you would miss all my imperfect ways
have no one to share all your imperfect days
if I could be different, I'd no longer be
the person I am, old imperfect me.

'Our imperfections are perfectly formed, why change them...'

MENOPAUSE THE WITCH

It comes over like a wave, you can see it in my eyes
you don't want to make things worse or antagonise
I'm snappy, taking offence at all the things you do
you won't respond, I'm doing wrong,
you say I know this isn't you
I'm irrational, hypersensitive or depressed
then manically industrious, not to mention stressed
But you know me, the largest part,
you say I'm beautiful and kind
you tell me that I'm gorgeous and perfectly designed
It's hard when menopause the witch is on patrol
but you know that in those moments I'm out of my control
You've tried your best to empathise you've the patience of a saint
you allow for days I'm not myself and do without complaint
At last the witch is leaving,
her invasion so unfair
that you allowed for that imposter,
shows how much you truly care.

'I was hijacked by the witch,
but the good fairy saw her off...'

FIGHTING THE INVADER

Hello, weird and abstinent invader
careless fool and ugly crusader
you were taking many unsuspecting souls
your presence now discovered
and discovered are your goals
Numbers we are many, combined in force to fight
with mental wellness on its way
for those that cry at night
no longer do we suffer in silence or disgrace
we are beating your invasion,
the war is taking place
Happy are we now you are derailed
mental wellness dominates and all that that entails
you can't escape, we have you trapped,
communication wins
the more we understand of you,
the more salvation brings
Striking you through cyberspace,
even striking you at home
the more we talk and empathise,
the more we're not alone
Strength in numbers, that's the key,
our army growing more
therapies of many kinds may one day make a cure.

'Unity is strength,
find strength in unity'

FORGIVE ME

Oh, forgive me, we've not long met,
you barely know my name
but there's something I must tell you,
as you may not feel the same
You're clearly taken by me, I also find you sprite
I need to tell of my condition
I only think it right
I wish that I could show you
like a bump or random rash
the condition that I speak of
may have you leaving in a dash
Bipolar, there I've said it,
I'm awaiting your response
not the sort of thing you say
when meeting only once
But if I don't make it clear to you,
you could later think me fraud
it took me so much courage, I hope there is reward
You smiled at me, you took my hand,
you were gentle in response
you commended me for honesty
and left the room at once!
Bum Bum

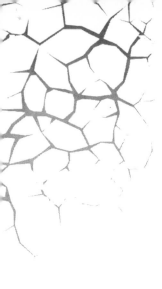

'Humour helps,
especially when you can laugh at
yourself'

YOU COULDN'T MAKE IT UP

I was crazy, everyone told me so
I was either can't be bothered or go go go
Extremely funny, the girls loved a night with me
or a nightmare honey for my husband left to see
Crying, life so dreadful, then singing in the bars
working several businesses or closing down for hours
I tried the patience of a saint, my family left agog
wondering what was wrong with me
and finding it a slog
I was always doing something, amazing or a drag
I had to find a balance, had to get it in the bag
It took me years but eventually
I sought the help I'd need
it takes courage and commitment to finally succeed
But crazy is as crazy does,
at least now it is controlled
I kept my own identity, now my story can be told.

'It's hard to operate
outside of the truth
and so liberating when you own it'

SEVENTEEN

I'm only seventeen, what have I seen, nothing
I sit around, lonely at times, feeling disgusting
Still in my pjs, nothing to dress for
hearing my mother, calling for some chore
I should be up and out with my friends
I don't really have any, I only pretend
I'm always alone, not part of the crowd
see me! I silently call aloud
I'm tired, sick of tears that I wipe
It's not really them, but myself I dislike
I'm depressed and anxiety wins
I try to explain but self-doubt begins
Afraid for my future and what I'll become
will I grow out of depression or will I succumb?
I cry for help, but nobody hears
Confirming I'm worthless and cementing my fears.

'Replacing fear with faith
Is hard
but you're never too young to try'

THE YOUNG

Oh, my granddaughter, such a beautiful girl
she suffers depression, so young, what a world
It seemed never to happen when I was a boy
depression not heard of in the young, not at all
It saddens me so to see her so anxious
I struggle to help her, my efforts so thankless
It helps her not to have others just scold her
I watch from the sides and I know I'll remain there
She's so lovely, a star and a jewel
depression has stolen her self-worth, it's so cruel
If all I can do is persist and remind her
how beautifully God in his wisdom designed her
I will be at her side as she walks on this journey
to conquer depression and prove herself worthy.

'Family matters,
what matters is family'

CONTROL

You will grow tired of inane accusations
the distorting of truth, those insinuations
They look for, set you up for, hypothetical situations
lay blame at your door for their interpretations
Cold and feel nothing when you're forced to crumble
they triumph, take pleasure in watching you stumble
Trying to convince you it's for your own good
they do it to help you, they're calling it love
Refuse to hear when you try to explain
that their behaviour is hurting you, causing you pain
No longer hurt yourself, trying to defend yourself
Your justification, they will never allow themselves
Unhealthy, destructive, it's not good for the soul
ask yourself, can you leave their control?

'Healthy self-esteem and confidence lead us to positive self-empowerment'

A DATE IN THE DIARY

I'm looking, I see it, my appointment is set
it's a date in the diary till my appointment is met
How will I play it, cool nothing wrong with me?
or reel off concerns so the doctor will see
that there is something missing or infecting my mind
or the prognosis, been nothing to find
This date in my diary has me anxious, I can't rest
now the appointment is made, it is for the best
at least that's what my family have said
I'll do it for them, then I've put it to bed
what if this date in my diary is just what I need?
the road to recovery or at least a reprieve
Okay, I'm going, I'll do this for them
no backing out, they'll only condemn
I owe them, they've suffered enough
this date in my diary a commitment of love
I'm telling myself anything to get me there
this date in my diary, the end of despair.

'Commitment is staying true to your word and your word remaining true to your actions'

BOADICEA

I made a friend a gorgeously crazy lady
wacky and wild, a real who loves ya baby
She was sharp, as sharp as a blade
didn't beat herself up for mistakes that she made
Laughed in the face of defeat if it came
and cursed the arrival of help just the same
She could quietly cause a major disaster
then light up the room with her joy and her laughter
A powerhouse, and at times a reclusive
a darling, who could turn very abusive
but what a teacher, not for the faint hearted
disguising her fears in the fights that she started
A winner, survivor a real Boadicea
if ever in trouble you know she'd appear
unconventional and very intelligent
kind, but with no time for sentiment
her mind often played tricks with her vibe
scars from her past where she often would hide
but wow, she could kick that to the curb
I admired her resolve, her come back superb
she's long in my past but the memories clear
of that wonderful woman, that real Boadicea.

'I don't suffer craziness
I enjoy every minute'

THE SECRET I KEEP

I won't say a word, the secret I keep
I don't see you by day, but you come in my sleep
not a dream but a nightmare that only I see
the pain is not yours, it stays here with me
I don't say your name or say what you did
I deny you the power and fear I forbid
I survived you, I won though I continue to fight
I'll never give in to the nightmares at night
The person I become is no testament to you
but the fight in my heart and the truth that I knew.

A determined spirit danced in the
rain and so,
took back the power that tried
causing the pain'

HORRID EPISODE

Such insanity, depression,
such hurtful words and attitude
the drama I bring with me, my desperate episodes
This craziness inside me, this rampant domicile
that resides in me so terribly,
takes my normal for a while
I'll smooth things over when I'm finding more control
apologise, they'll sympathise,
I'll promise healing as my goal
What sends this ball in motion,
is there something sets me off
this ballad of commotion, in this emotional trough
Now celebrating, captivating, utterly exhilarating,
finally annihilating beating my distress,
but I know this kind of ecstasy, is only danger in a dress
Where to find my equilibrium,
where to find my balanced mind
will there ever be an answer
to these questions I've combined?

'Confusion is only a temporary absence of reason'

REMEMBER ME

Remember me fondly, I'm not far away
I could never just leave you
I just couldn't stay
I was tired, I was ready to kiss you goodbye
please don't torture yourself, by asking God why
There're reminders of me in the words of a song
or the breeze on your cheek as you're walking along
I'm the leaves that surround you when winter is near
carrying whispers that only you hear
and the rain as it falls and you're unprepared
so I'm able to cover you as much as I dare
I can be near you whenever I see
the longing in you for the longing of me
so, don't fret like you do, though my body is gone
My love and my soul still linger on
I live in your heart.

'That moment when we realise we
can't touch, but we feel'

WHATEVER

Hey counsellor! you therapist, you champion of the mind
you can look inside that book, but me you'll never find
I'm young, I'm dismissing you,
what do my parents know?
Talking is so stupid, I will always tell them so
no one can identify with my crazy hyper energy
dismissed at home, dismissed at school,
seems a double jeopardy
Decreased motivation and disorganisation,
that could be anyone?
Avoidance, unaware of consequence,
well isn't that everyone
I'm not easy to know, not easy to handle,
not easy to position
I pretend not to care and pretend not to hear
their endless repetition
I'm struggling in my teenage self,
who am I meant to be
Your handing out drugs and labels
like Asperger's and ADHD
maybe I'll humour you and go along with what you say
Hey councillor, I could prove you wrong,
or I'll be thanking you some day.

'Sometimes it's not easy to listen
and even harder to talk'

EMOTIONAL AMPLIFIER

Celebrating, captivating, utterly exhilarating
finally annihilating, finally free
Cultivating, harnessing positivity
accumulating, demonstrating everything that's me
Depleted, defeated, utterly deleted
why would anybody listen to me?
Totally, cheated, I have now retreated
hiding, retiring, hot and perspiring
I absolutely hate being me
Soothing, not losing, regaining liberty
refraining now from inability
The emotional amplifier, that is me.

'Emotional agility
the brains capability'

ONE STEP AT A TIME

When faced with a mountain,
think of a hill
then one step at a time
means climb it you will
Not in a day,
maybe not in a year
but each step that you take
is that one step nearer
Tiredness isn't weakness
and tears not just for joy
to cry and rest releases stress
and hopelessness destroys
So trust yourself with patience,
commit yourself to win
deal in only victories
that you yourself begin
For each tiny step that's taken,
uphill taken slow
will rise you even higher
than you ever thought you'd go.

Be the phoenix, rise from the ashes
because you can'

ACROSS THE ROOM

I saw you far across the room
a handsome face yet all alone
Though many people circled you
your presence there, not wanting too
Misplaced, I fear you don't belong
you're singing someone else's song
Saddened by your loneliness
I wonder why your heart's distressed
We haven't met, yet your face a story told
of happiness yet to unfold
I sigh, for I recognise
that lost to all, that sad disguise
I too sing to another's tune
trapped like you across the room.

'If you don't like the music
Sing your own song'

TO YOU TO ME

I have reached the point of no return
perhaps you'll never understand
My pain too great to linger here
no chance for me, I'm damned
Consumed by loathing you don't see
I fight the demons in my mind
I have no fear; relief is near
my pain be gone, yet yours to find.

We find you, how cruel
how shattered are our lives?
to find you gone in such a way
our desperate crying asking why
your legacy our deep despair
now no chance to say goodbye
our love our care was always there
and yet you chose to die

If we could only rewind time
and save you from yourself
show you how tomorrow looked
with chance with change with help

'It wasn't really his life that he wanted to end, but his life as he knew it'

break the barrier

MATTER of MIND

My lovely friend so full of life
he was wide in girth and 6ft 5 in height
Lived in the moment and cherished his time
filled it with hobbies, often joining in mine
Then slowly, forgetting, misplacing, reminiscing
searching my eyes for the bits that were missing
Slowly but surely, I watched him leave
a lonely retreat and hard to believe
Dementia, the thief stealing my friend
waging a war that he couldn't defend
I could never desert him, he had to be homed
so I sat with him often, while his mind roamed
I'd hold onto his hand and smile to his eyes
tell him I loved him through tears that he cried
I'm sure that a flicker of him lingered on
right to the end, only then was he gone
Grateful my friend now resting in peace
from the grip of dementia, a welcome release.

'Vacant doesn't mean empty'

PERSPECTIVE

Where is the perspective
when all rational thoughts are gone
and your interpretation
is dismissed by everyone?
Sifting through the rubbish
accumulated in the brain
inner chimp is out of cage
and will not be tamed
Breathe deep, recall the words
meant to calm and sooth
diminish frustration
and the anger too remove
Don't make reality anything other than it is
we won't avoid disfunction
in her life, yours or his
But this need to gain perspective
is a fundamental right
a verbal explanation,
the mind's clarity of sight
It takes equalised emotions
for rationale to win the day
then a gaining of perspective
leads to sense in what we say.

It's those worries and fears that override our rational thinking

BALANCE RESTORED

Wow, this is a brilliant day
no matter the weather,
no matter it's grey
the sunshine within me
is like the brightest in May
All is in balance,
my family and planets aligned
they go about their day,
as I go about mine
It is easy to see
why we all rub along
it's our world
and where we belong
No major issues,
no problems to solve
no one anxious or down,
no disputes to resolve
Yes, I'll take happy,
oh what a blast
balance restored,
and long may it last.

'Being happy is like being content
with knobs on'

YOU CAN

If you can't change your situation
change it by the way you perceive
your thoughts become words you eventually believe
Resist and persist can be fairly exchanged
acceptance brings freedom and the power for change
Shrink down negative thoughts and visualise
imagine them shrinking in power and size
Self-love, the first to renew
exploring the things that bring pleasure to you
What you need to hear from others, say to yourself
independence, in your emotional health
You can take control, your mission is possible
your welfare imperative, your spirit phenomenal.

'You can
You will'

WHEN YOU LEFT

If I only knew how your passing would feel
the pain was abhorrent and hard to conceal
I wasn't prepared, you were stolen from us
It happened so quickly, what was the rush?
Why you? I cried, why did it have to be you?
we needed you here, you had much left to do
As the pain that we felt left us more than bereft
this hideous crime, this humongous theft
Angry and feral the cries came from me
night followed day to an endless degree
Praying and crying did nothing to ease
the pain left in our hearts, for your heart's disease
How couldn't we know, how did we miss
this harmful disease in someone so fit?
A dangerous cover, it discriminates not
the heart in the body, then the body is not
I held our son in my arms never wishing to stop
for his heart was so broken for the father he lost
But you can be proud of the man he's become
because you were his father and he is your son
It comforts us now to believe you are near
as time passes by, we still think of you here
Just working away on some beautiful plain
watching, still caring, till we see you again.

'The heart is formidable
it holds so many people'

THE MAN BEHIND THE MASK

I'm a geezer, hardnosed and a grafter
I stand at the bar and join in the laughter
An uncle, a brother, a cousin and son
the apple of my parents' eyes, especially my mum
Yes, I'm a geezer so I keep up my guard
no one must see me, just the man that is hard
Here in the space of my own home
I sit and I sink, feeling very alone
Left at the bar is the geezer charade
here on my own I cry from the heart
In the grip of depression so physically strong
how did I get it, where did I go wrong?
It's stronger at times than all might in me
I'd rather be beaten by someone I can see
But this sneak hide's, waiting its chance
it takes from behind, a coward with a lance
Glad that no one can witness or see
me in depression, brought to my knees
I hide this, it's weak, I despise it
better to wait till I'm able to disguise it
No doctor's tablets, no counsellor's fee
I'm the man in the mask, that man is me.

'Mental illness doesn't
discriminate'

DUVET DAY

I don't care what the weather is doing
I'm fed up, but I'm warm and I'm not moving
I don't care who knocks at the door
they'll come back if they've been here before
The postman can leave me a note if he wishes
the kitchen can stay with its unwashed dishes
No husband or kids, no needs to attend to
only mine and I don't need or intend to
Don't care I'm not up nor put a brush to my hair
or opened the window, no need for fresh air
No TV, no music, just the soft ruffled sound
that comes from my duvet as I tug it around
Nothing will faze me, I'm hiding today
here in my bed with my lovely duvet.

'Switching off takes guts'

YESTERDAY

Oh, I think I've blown it,
my ranting's deranged, and I knew it
But I had no control, I was verbally violent
it was nothing to me, but to them incoherent
Today I don't think I can face them at all
nowhere to hide they're just down the hall
Sorry won't cut it, we've been here before
I wish I could take myself, walk out the door
No escape for me, it must be faced
apologies, I am a disgrace
Face them I do, they are looking so hurt
what makes it worse, they never desert
They stick with me though I'm such a disgrace
they know my condition, they know what I face
Yesterday happened, it's been an age since I dipped
apologies yesterday, it seemed that I flipped
The love that they have for me never let's go
I'm sorry they know it and they want me to know
Yesterday happened, let's go forward they say
I'm regretful for yesterday and so grateful today.

'Just when we think we've nailed it,
we get a reminder!
it's called honing our skills'

SWITCHING THE FILES

My mind is my office, I'm head of the board
my thinking is filed and the categories stored
Organised chaos is sometimes the way
if my filing's undone at the end of the day
I have various folders with various files
some are quite anxious and others are trials
I have to make sure those files stay apart
or confusion is all that will flow on my chart
Categories include anxiety, depression
with feelings of doubt despair or obsession
but others are filled full of positive files
creative, go getting, that self-reconcile
replacing those files filled with fear or with doubt
and placing in letters of courage throughout
With practice it works and I'm clearer of mind
how great that the folders and files were designed.

'Don't like what you're thinking
replace it with something you do'

MY PRAYER

I can't speak,
my grief a sob and a prayer
as my heart breaks
and I picture you there
I'm caressing a jumper
that still holds your smell
now sodden with tears
I have no wish to quell
My sadness so bleak,
my loneliness and sorrow
my prayer,
that the Lord will return you tomorrow.

'We always ask the impossible when the impossible has happened'

MY BODY SPOKE ITS MIND

I was ashamed I had an illness, I tried so hard to deny
to myself I'd distort the truth, convinced by my own lie
My body would defend itself, my ailments testament
to my frenetic habits and to my detriment
Reprisal or ridicule were waiting I feared
another burden on the mind for my body to hear
Sleepless nights, frantic days, my eyes heavy with defeat
against the mental illness and the symptoms, it repeats
My body was saying my mind's in distress
if I could find words that my voice could express
If I could be brave and tell someone who'd care
so, I could seek help in my helpless despair
My laptop became my private resource
where I privately searched and I privately talked
My cyber angels that lived in my screen
saved me from suffering more than I deemed
My insight much clearer, I wasn't alone
my ailments retreated, my mind was my own.

'If the body suffers, the mind needs to listen,
listen to the wisdom of your body'

POUNDING HEART

I'm sweating, I'm starting to tremble and shake
I feel sick, the knots in my stomach aren't fake
They sit there like rocks, I can't breathe
my heart is pounding, there's no reprieve
It's like I'm being attacked but there's nobody here
there's no need to panic, there's nothing to fear
Yet I'm fearful
I'm frightened there's no one to call
there is, but they'll think I've lost it, once and for all
I'm crying, this is crippling now
make it stop, I wish I knew how
How long does it last, I can't perceive?
Finally… relief, head down, I'm starting to breathe
Oh, what the hell was that
that was anxiety, a panic attack.

Closed eyes, deep breaths, calm
your world from within'

BEAUTIFUL SOULS

Beautiful souls have known fear, suffering and have often been lo
some journeyed without comfort and at great personal cost
Just themselves to depend, defend and finally rescue
they a chrysalis metamorphosis, transforming into
Caring and kindness, empathy, support and encouragement
when they identify in others the need for such nourishment
Yes, beautiful souls never just happen
they are made up from suffering turned into compassion.

'Real beauty is soul deep'

FROM THE MOUTHS OF BABES

They say that from the mouth of babes
and isn't that the truth
everything you do or say, they see and learn from you
One day when we were playing,
he stopped and stared at me
and what he said determined the change that had to be
Mummy, here's a plaster I'm putting on your heart
I sometimes hear you crying
and I want to help you stop
I love you, Mummy, don't be sad,
I will make you better
I even asked for Santa's help when writing him my letter
I stemmed the tears from falling
as I took him in my arms
I closed my eyes and promised him
his letter worked a charm
For the words that he had written
and the plaster now in place
would stop my tears from falling
and keep a smile upon my face
Please don't worry, Son, when Mummy cries,
it's sometimes cries of joy
for God gave me the biggest gift in you, my baby boy.

'You can't kid a kid'

TURN AWAY

False faces speak false truth to hear
like fools they deal in false veneer
Much joy it brings to see you down
a smile for them, for you a frown
Such puffed up chest, such confidence
when watching fall your competence
These no-good fiends hold not for you
your downfall, their breath renew
Don't hold with them, you must disregard
their false truth and game facade
Be done, best turn your face away
let not them harm your heart today.

'You have to meet the fake to understand the forgery, then value the lesson'

DON'T

Don't apologise without knowing what you did wrong
Don't try explain to someone when they're dismissive or try
string you along
Don't question your belief or opinions because they don't
match with someone else
Don't give away your power under threat, or any passive
aggression dealt
Don't allow anyone to give motives to your actions when the
opposite was your intention
Don't allow anyone to make you feel small or ashamed or
inflict on you any limitation
Don't fear your word before you speak, that's someone
taking your
freedom
And don't ever deny who you are or give up your dreams for
any other's reason
You don't need to stay in a false reality
you're you, with your own beautiful, unique personality.

'Don't give power to your doubt'

HEY MAN

Take off that mask the world made you wear
it's hell, you're conditioned to keep silent despair
You've been programmed
to think that strength is denial
denying your struggle, forcing your smile
You don't want to look weak, you don't want to burden
that mask is stopping you talk, your feelings uncertain
Or worse, you're scaring yourself
with the darkest of thoughts
staying there in denial with the sadness it's brought
Hey man, your feelings are real and it's okay to cry
your courage is hidden by society's lie
You're more than you are, allowed, told or valued to be
speak out, your strength be revealed, set yourself free
Hey man, this is you, all of you combined
no need to hide your feelings, you're perfectly defined.

'faking it isn't making it'

ANGEL BABY

My darling angel baby not destined for my arms
all I have of you an image
inside me, safe from harm
But God changed his mind
and chose to keep you in his care
you must have been that angel
he just couldn't bear to share
I knew when you had ceased to thrive,
I know I felt you leave
that I would never hold my baby,
was just too hard to believe
I imagine you're that shining star,
that constant in the sky
reminding me you're out there
in that world that never dies
I loved you so my darling,
my love is wanting still
for the day that I may hold you,
as I believe I will.

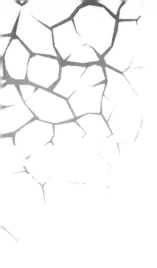

'Our unborn Angels
our own heavenly stars'

SILENCE

No need for cliché words
for me to feel special or unique
though my mind at time deceives me,
my heart the truth will speak
Fluent in silence,
not quite the language of my choice
but no interpretation needed
for the sounds within my voice
If loneliness compounded when people all around
then contentment and at peace
when sat with nature and it's sounds
No need to share opinions, my opinions are my own
cultivated knowledge
through the world that I have known
Emotions travel through me
though self-pity has no place
I appreciate all contact with a smile upon my face
My choice to value words I hear,
my choice to let them go
my silence isn't absence is all you need to know.

'The power of the unspoken word,
in a world full of chatter'

THREE THINGS

I count three things at the end of each day that have made me feel h
just simple things, nothing wowing or wacky
The child in my arms or a kiss from husband
a walk with the dog who's so loving and trusting
It may be a stranger who opened the door
after seeing me struggle with shopping instore
Or the smell of the washing all folded and nice
and the sun through the window all glowing and bright
The hug from my son as he comes home from college
whose mind is so open and hungry for knowledge
As I look in the eyes of the family who love me
I'm grateful I'm here and not where I could be
Three things, stop me from stressing
and helps me to focus on all of my blessings.

'Being grateful is grounding'

YOU HAVE ALREADY WON

Remember that time when you thought you were truly beat
you had nowhere to turn, you resigned yourself to defeat
That was a dark time and it wasn't the first
your struggles in life have left their scars and they hurt
but you won, you came through
those skies, so grey, eventually turned blue
Your strength within never let you down
your smile eventually took your frown
that was you, and nobody else
You dealt with those nightmares and all by yourself
you harness support, you gravitate with a will to survive
You're a winner and that's why you're alive
and living, with the wisdom that you will overcome
anything, just like those battles you have already won.

'you don't just win once'

FIGHT

What a strong word, how empowering,
how delightful do I feel
when I fight my old intruder,
my prize, my spirit healed
It's not easy for a moment,
it's not easy for a time
it's fantastically achieving
and the victory is mine
I won't pay that awful ransom,
I won't lose what's rightfully mine
I will always be obnoxious
in the face of my decline
I will save me from disaster,
I will save me from it all
I will consciously inspire myself
and keep me standing tall
It won't define me with a title,
it won't determinedly declare
a war on me so brutal
that leaves me lying there
for I will constantly defy it,
I will constantly reframe
as I acknowledge this my illness
and beat it all the same

Yes, I am empowered
even though you do reside
I make you sit and wait your chance
denying you your ride
You are powerless today
and will be powerless tomorrow
you will lie in wait but never make
my sadness or my sorrow.
So, fight I will and fight is still
a strong, and powerful word
that keeps me straight and fearless
in this fearful anxious world.

'Win battles,
but never be at war
with yourself'

Our mental health is our emotional, psychological and social well-being. If you or someone you love has been affected by mental health issues and would like help, with permission I have added the following contact information.

www.mind.org.uk/information-support/a-z-mental-health

When you're living with a mental health problem, or supporting someone who is, having access to the
right information about a condition, treatment options, or practical issues – is vital.

www.lindajthorne.com